AI for Musicians:

How to Create a Website That Rocks

Contents

Hi, I'm Steve Smythe, a musician and tech nerd.

I've been a musician for over thirty years and a techie for just as long. While I enjoy all the time I spend playing music, it's not my full-time job. I have a decades-long career in technology, software, websites, and digital marketing.

My passion for the two has led me down a unique path, one where I could be ahead of the game. Playing music and growing with technology, sticking with both, and becoming an expert along the way. Now, music and tech are second nature to me.

Though, I know that this is not the case with everybody. If you're reading this book, you are probably already a musician, but you may not be a tech expert. Technology is an ever-changing field, and that can be scary and daunting, but it shouldn't be a roadblock. I'm here to let you know that it's not too late to become an expert yourself.

I believe technology and music are meant to be together. They are both inspiring, unique, and dynamic forces constantly acting to move the world forward. When AI was introduced to the masses, I had already been using it. So, I thought to myself, how can I use my experience to help my fellow musicians benefit from this new invention? How could I help my fellow musicians spread their music and their bands properly onto the internet to bolster their success? That's exactly why I wrote this book, to show you how. You can find me at www.smyco.me, and look me up on social media too. I would be happy to answer any questions and assist you in any way I can.

So, without further ado, get to learning!

I sincerely hope you enjoy,

Steve

Chapter 1

Introduction to AI and Its Benefits for Your Music Website

Are you a musician who wants to create a music website that is truly unique and unforgettable?

If so, you need to consider using artificial intelligence (AI). AI is a powerful tool that can help you create compelling stories and engaging content for your music website.

Here are a few ways that AI can help you create a more engaging music website:

- AI can help you write a compelling bio. AI can analyze your music and create a bio that is both informative and engaging. This will help you connect with potential fans and get them excited about your music. For example, the AI platform Bard can generate text that is both creative and informative.

Here is an example of how AI can be used to write a compelling bio for a musician:

"I am a singer-songwriter who has been writing music since I was a child. I am inspired by the natural world and the human experience. My music is a reflection of my love for both. I am passionate about using my music to connect with people and make a difference in the world."

This bio is informative because it tells the reader about the musician's background, their musical influences, and their passion for music. It is also engaging because it is written in a clear and concise way, and it uses vivid language to paint a picture of the musician's life and work.

- AI can help you create a story for your band or solo project. AI can generate stories that are based on your music and your experiences. This will help you create a more personal connection with your fans and make your music more relatable. For example, the AI platform Storysmith can generate stories that are both engaging and thought-provoking.

Here is an example of how AI can be used to create a story for a band:

The band was formed in a small town in the Midwest. The members were all friends who loved music and wanted to create something special. They started out playing small gigs in local bars, but they quickly gained a following. Their music was raw and emotional, and it resonated with people from all walks of life.

The band eventually moved to Los Angeles to pursue their dream of making it big. They signed with a record label and released their debut album. The album was a success, and the band quickly became one of the most popular bands in the world.

The band's music has inspired people all over the world. They have helped people to connect with their emotions and to find their voice. They are a reminder that anything is possible if you follow your dreams.

This story is engaging because it is well-written and it is easy to relate to. It is also thought-provoking because it raises questions about the power of music and the importance of following your dreams.

- AI can help you write blog posts and articles about your music. AI can research topics related to your music and write blog posts and articles that are informative and interesting. This will help you establish yourself as an expert in your field and attract new fans. For example, the AI platform Jasper can generate text that is both factual and engaging.

Here is an example of how AI can be used to write a blog post about music:

The history of music is a long and winding one. It has evolved over time, and it has been influenced by different cultures and traditions. Today, there are many different genres of music, each with its own unique sound.

One of the most popular genres of music is pop music. Pop music is typically characterized by catchy melodies, simple lyrics, and a focus on rhythm. It is a genre that appeals to a wide audience, and it is often used to promote products and services.

Another popular genre of music is rock music. Rock music is typically characterized by loud guitars, powerful vocals, and a rebellious attitude. It is a genre that has been associated with social change and protest.

No matter what your musical taste is, there is sure to be a genre of music that you enjoy. Music is a powerful force that can connect people from all walks of life. It can inspire, motivate, and entertain. So next time you're looking for something to listen to, why not explore different genres of music and see what you find?

This blog post is informative because it provides a brief overview of the history of music and the different genres of music that exists today. It is also engaging because it uses vivid language and interesting facts to keep the reader's attention.

These are just a few of the ways that AI can be used to create a more engaging music website. AI is a powerful tool that can help you to tell your story,

Chapter 2

Comparing Website Builders and Choosing the Right One for Your Music Website

Introduction to Musicians' Online Presence

In today's digital world, having an online presence is crucial for musicians to build their fanbase and promote their artistry. A website serves as the hub that brings together all aspects of a musician's brand - their bio, music, merch, shows, press, and more.

In this chapter, we will explore the evolution of websites for musicians, from early basic pages to modern AI-powered experiences. We'll look at how artificial intelligence is transforming website creation and management. A detailed comparison of leading website builder platforms will break down their features, capabilities, and pricing. Real-world case studies will show how musicians are using these tools. Finally, we'll review key factors to consider when selecting the right website builder for your music career goals and budget.

The Growing Significance of Websites for Musicians

Just two decades ago, musicians were still debating if they even needed a website. In the early 2000s, websites were seen more as a novelty than a necessity. But fast forward to today in 2023, and a website is considered one of the most fundamental elements of a musician's online toolkit.

Websites have become essential for musicians for several key reasons:

Control of Branding - A website gives musicians full control over their visual branding style. This allows them to stand out and present a professional look that represents their artistry.

Hub for All Activity - Websites function as a central hub that connects all of a musician's online activities across different platforms and social media sites. Fans can go to the website to access everything in one place.

Promoting Music - A website makes it easy for fans to listen to music, view videos, and learn about new releases. Musicians can provide lyrics, liner notes, concert footage, and more.

Selling Merchandise - With built- informal capabilities, websites allow musicians to easily sell physical and digital merchandise directly to fans.

Marketing Shows and Events - Websites give musicians a way to list tour dates, promote upcoming shows, and even sell tickets.

Data and Analytics - Using visitor data and analytics, musicians can understand fan behavior and optimize their website effectively.

Without a website, musicians are missing out on ownership over their brand identity, connection with fans, and revenue opportunities. However, just having any website is not enough. Musicians must choose the right platform and leverage the capabilities available today.

Evolution of Music Websites: From Humble Beginnings to Sophisticated AI

The earliest musician websites in the mid-90s were very limited. Most used simple HTML code to present basic text bios, discographies, and tour dates. Some added low-resolution images and clunky MIDI music files.

The limitations of early web technology meant sites were mostly informational, without much interactive content.

By the early 2000s, musician websites became more advanced, using CSS for styled layouts and incorporating multimedia like photos, audio, and video. Many musicians used site builders like GeoCities and Angelfire to customize templates and themes. However, website creation still required manually editing code or using confusing interfaces.

The late 2000s brought the rise of content management systems like WordPress and Drupal. These simplified the process of building and updating sites with modular plugins and themes. Musicians could now easily manage dynamic content including blogs, galleries, and user comments. Mobile responsiveness became important as smartphone usage grew.

Today in 2023, artificial intelligence is revolutionizing the way musicians build and manage their websites:

- AI site builders like Wix ADI create responsive designs instantly just by answering questions.

- Personalized recommendations allow for easy customization matching musicians' styles.

- Built-in SEO and analytics optimize sites to help fans discover content.

- Features like merch stores and mailing lists integrate directly.

- Chatbots and virtual assistants enhance visitor experiences.

- Automated content creation drafts compelling bios, discographies, and blog posts.

Let's take a deeper look at how artificial intelligence is transforming modern website platforms.

Understanding the Role of AI in Website Builders

Artificial intelligence now plays an integral role in how both general and music-specific website builders operate. AI capabilities embedded in these platforms aim to make website creation easy for musicians with minimal technical skills.

So how exactly does AI enhance website builders? **Here are some of the key ways:**

Smart Templates - AI analyzers evaluate visual trends, color palettes, and layouts that align with a musician's preferred styles. This allows generating design templates that uniquely match the brand.

Facilitating Personalization - Based on user behaviors and preferences, AI can automatically customize navigation, page layouts, featured content and recommendations for each visitor.

Drafting Content - AI can generate original text content like bios, discographies, and blog posts by prompting with keywords, topics, and tone parameters. Musicians can then edit before publishing.

SEO Optimization - AI evaluates pages and recommends improvements to titles, headers, meta descriptions, alt text, and structure to optimize for search engine visibility.

Accessibility Checking - AI can scan websites to detect issues impacting users with disabilities like low vision or hearing loss, then provide fixes.

Monitoring Performance - AI tracks meaningful metrics like page loads, bounce rates, conversions, and sales to provide actionable insights.

Chatbots & Virtual Assistants - AI powers conversational interfaces to engage visitors and help answer common questions.

These capabilities showcase how integral AI now is for building fully functional, well-optimized websites tailored to each musician's brand and goals.

Key Benefits of AI Website Builders for Musicians

Let's explore some of the key benefits musicians can realize by leveraging artificial intelligence features on modern website building platforms:

Quick Setup - Even musicians with minimal design or coding skills can launch beautiful, professional-looking websites within hours or minutes using AI templates.

Easy Customization - AI allows for easy drag-and-drop editing and modifications to tailor pages to your brand personality and musical aesthetic.

Ongoing Optimization - AI continually provides data-driven suggestions to improve website layout, content, and performance based on how visitors interact.

Targeted Engagement - AI personalization ensures visitors see relevant content, products, and recommendations aligned to their interests and behavior.

SEO Visibility - AI gives constant guidance to maintain on-page and technical SEO, improving organic search visibility.

Accessibility - AI tools help remove barriers for visitors with disabilities to access and comfortably use websites.

Workload Reduction - AI can automate tasks like content generation, analytics, security monitoring and backups that take up time.

Lower Cost - AI website builders reduce the need for separate tools, developers, designers - allowing huge savings.

Having AI handle time-consuming website tasks allows musicians to focus on creating music and engaging with fans, not wrestling with technology.

AI Features to Look For in Website Builders

When evaluating website builders for musicians, look for these key AI capabilities:

- AI Site Generator - Creates draft sites in minutes that can be edited and published instantly.

- Automatic Music Embedding - Allows adding songs/albums so fans can listen right on your site.

- Intelligent Merchandising - Dynamically recommend and promote your merch to fans based on interests and habits.

- SEO Optimization Tools - Check keyword usage, site speed, structure and provide guidance to improve visibility.

- Performance Analytics - Track meaningful engagement and sales metrics and get intelligent insights.

- Content Creation Tools - Assist writing compelling bios, discographies, and blog posts tailored to your brand voice.

- Chatbots & Virtual Assistants - Provide conversational experiences to engage visitors and assist with queries.

- Personalized Experiences - Customize site layout, content, product suggestions for each visitor.

- Accessibility Checking - Scan for issues that might affect disabled users and provide fixes.

- Security & Backup Monitoring - Automatically watch for threats and ensure regular backups.

Prioritizing these AI capabilities will ensure your website leverages the full power of artificial intelligence. But functionality is only one aspect of choosing a platform. Next, let's compare some top contenders.

Comparing Leading Website Builders for Musicians

Many website builders now cater specifically to musicians. Let's compare four popular options - Wix, Squarespace, Bandzoogle, and WordPress.

Wix

Wix empowers anyone to build sleek websites via drag and drop, even without coding skills. The AI-driven Wix ADI takes your preferences to instantly generate a customized site. Musicians can easily add audio, video, mailing lists, and merch stores. SEO and marketing tools built-in.

Key Strengths:

- AI site generator for fast launch

- Easy drag and drop editor

- Mobile optimized designs

- Hundreds of templates

- Built-in SEO and marketing

Potential Drawbacks:

- Can seem cluttered for beginners

- Limited design customization

- Add-ons and upgrades cost extra

- Must use Wix domain

Squarespace

Squarespace offers elegant designer-made templates, robust ecommerce, and integrated marketing tools. Powerful customization options plus 24/7 support. Ideal for music, video, blogs, and galleries.

Key Strengths:

- Beautiful modern templates

- Easy customization options

- Powerful built-in commerce

- Integrated email marketing

- Strong multimedia capabilities

Potential Drawbacks:

- Limited free plan options

- Steeper learning curve

- Templates can seem restrictive

Bandzoogle

Bandzoogle specializes in websites for musicians with tools tailored to promoting shows, music, and merch. Offers mobile-ready themes, mailing lists, and fan retention features. Designed for user-friendliness.

Key Strengths:

- Specialized for musicians

- Easy tour date management

- Integrated store for music and merch

- Fan club platform and email lists

- Hundreds of templates

Potential Drawbacks:

- Less design customization

- Fewer plug-ins compared to WordPress

- Caters only to musicians

WordPress

WordPress is the world's most popular CMS used by over 40% of websites. Offers ultimate customization using thousands of themes and plugins. Requires self-hosting but ideal for full control and scalability. More technical skill needed.

Key Strengths:

- Extremely customizable

- Huge theme and plugin ecosystem

- Open source and free software

- Scales to any size

- Very SEO-friendly

Potential Drawbacks:

- Steep learning curve

- Self-hosting required

- Must manage updates and security

- Less integrated features

Let's compare the AI capabilities of each platform:

Platform	AI Site Builder	Personalization	SEO Tools	Content Creator	Analytics	Chatbot Integration
Wix	Yes	Decent	Good	Minimal	Good	Yes
Squarespace	No	Good	Decent	No	Good	Third Party
Bandzoogle	No	Decent	Good	No	Decent	Third Party
WordPress	Plugins Available	Plugins Available	Plugins Available	Plugins Available	Plugins Available	Plugins Available

For ease of use, Wix leads with its AI site generator, while Squarespace offers greater design flexibility. Bandzoogle caters specifically to musicians. WordPress requires more work but allows advanced customization.

Now that we've compared the capabilities, let's break down the pricing and plans.

Comparing Pricing and Plans

Pricing can vary widely depending on the features and options you need. Here is an overview of the plans available across different platforms:

Wix

- Free - 500MB storage, 1GB bandwidth, Wix ad banner

- Combo - $14-24/month - 3GB storage, 2GB bandwidth, email marketing

- Unlimited - $24-49/month - Unlimited storage, bandwidth, videos, premium features

Squarespace

- Free Trial - 14 day free trial, full features

- Personal - $12-26/month - Unlimited storage, basic commerce

- Business - $26-40/month - Advanced commerce, email marketing, contributors

Bandzoogle

- Free Trial - 30 day free trial

- Basic - $8.29/month - 500MB storage, unlimited bandwidth

- Pro - $15.88/month - 2GB storage, unlimited videos, HD audio

- Elite - $27.46/month - 5GB storage, fan club platform, priority support

WordPress

- Free software but must pay for web hosting:

- Basic shared hosting - $5-25/month

- Managed WordPress hosting - $25-100+/month

When evaluating cost:

- Consider bandwidth needs for hosting media files which can require more resources.

- Factor in email list size which may require upgraded plans with higher limits.

- Assess ecommerce needs - occasional digital downloads vs. full online store.

- Determine required storage for hosting images, audio, video, and other media uploads.

- Evaluate the level of functionality, customization, and support needed.

- Weigh the cost vs long-term scalability as your career grows.

Study the details closely to select the right plan based on your budget, needs, and goals. Some providers offer short-term discounts for annual subscriptions. Don't lock yourself into a long-term plan if requirements might change. Now let's look at real examples of musicians using these website platforms.

Real-World Case Studies

To better understand how these website builders work in practice, let's look at examples of two musicians who created their sites using different platforms.

Case Study 1: Indie Folk Musician Using Wix

John Riley is an up-and-coming indie folk musician who needed an easy way to build a professional website to complement his recent EP release. As an independent artist, his budget was limited. He also lacked advanced technical skills for building a custom site from scratch.

After comparing his options, John decided to use Wix. He liked the artificial intelligence-driven features and extensive template library. Using the Wix ADI tool, he was able to launch a fully functioning site in under two hours. The site reflects his musical style with a simple, elegant, mobile-friendly design.

On his Wix site, John highlights audio samples from his new EP, embedded from Spotify. With Wix Ascend, he easily collected email subscribers. Using Velo by Wix, he set up a merch store to sell CDs and t-shirts. The built-in SEO tools help fans discover his site when searching for folk music in his region.

For around $20 per month, John now has a professional hub to direct fans to his music and events. The site analytics give data to optimize his content and grow his audience. Overall, the artificial intelligence capabilities in Wix met John's needs for an easy-to-use, budget-friendly website.

Case Study 2: Established Singer Using Squarespace

Jane Smith is an established jazz and blues singer with a dedicated fan base. However, her old website looked dated and was difficult to update. She wanted a new site with a stylish design aligned to her brand aesthetic. It also had to showcase her music catalog and allow selling merchandise.

After researching options tailored to artists and musicians, she chose Squarespace. With Squarespace's range of beautiful templates, Jane found it easy to create an on-brand look reflecting her retro, artistic style. Using custom CSS, she tweaked fonts, colors, and layouts to differentiate from other sites.

Jane populated her site with samples from her latest album, along with videos from past live performances. The integrated Squarespace Commerce let her easily sell special edition vinyl records and apparel. Email marketing tools like Segment help Jane identify and re-engage fans who have lapsed.

Thanks to Jane's new Squarespace website, she has a scalable platform ready to grow along with her expanding career. The extensive customization options enabled her to dial in the perfect representation of her personal brand identity.

These real-world examples showcase how musicians leverage website builders in different ways. Wix offered John simplicity for his basic needs, while Squarespace provided Jane more complex capabilities.

Key Considerations When Choosing a Website Platform

When selecting a website builder, musicians should weigh several factors carefully based on their specific situation and goals:

- Skill level - Pick a platform that matches your technical proficiency. If you are less experienced, choose options like Wix for easy use. For advanced skills, select WordPress for limitless customization.

- Design flexibility - Certain builders like Squarespace offer more ways to customize design and layout. Evaluate if you need extended options to uniquely brand your site.

- Budget - Compare pricing tiers based on traffic needs, email list size, ecommerce plans, and resources required. But also weigh long-term value.

- Music integration - If showcasing your songs directly on your site is a priority, ensure the platform facilitates audio and video embedding.

- Marketing capabilities - Determine what native SEO, email, and social media integration you need built-in versus using third-party add-ons.

- Support options - Review if the provider offers sufficient self-help resources, community forums, or dedicated customer support.

- Scalability - Consider future growth plans and how easily the platform and your plan can scale up as your career evolves.

- Ownership - Some like Wix restrict you to using their domain. Others like WordPress allow registering your own custom domain name.

Taking the time to thoroughly evaluate these key factors against your needs and constraints will help zero in on the ideal platform. If still undecided, sign up for free trials to test options firsthand.

Conclusion

Creating a website today is essential for musicians to promote their craft, engage fans, and drive revenue. The meteoric rise of artificial intelligence is transforming how musicians build, manage and optimize their websites.

AI capabilities like smart site generation, data-driven recommendations, personalized experiences, SEO improvements, automated content creation, chatbots, and more allow websites to deliver much greater value with less effort.

Top website building platforms like Wix, Squarespace, Bandzoogle, and WordPress enable musicians to launch stylish, functional sites faster than ever before. Comparing factors like pricing, support, design flexibility, and music integration helps determine the best choice.

Leveraging AI technology allows musicians to focus less on website mechanics and devote more energy to their real passion - making music. A custom-tailored site serves as the digital hub bringing together all aspects of their brand and career.

With strategic planning and the right platform choice, musicians can use their website as a core asset for reaching fans, growing their audience, and monetizing their artistry.

Chapter 3

How to Choose the Right Features for Your Music Website

Introduction

A musician's website serves many purposes - promoting their music, attracting new fans, engaging with supporters, selling merchandise, and more. With so many potential features to choose from, how do you determine the right set for your goals?

In this chapter, we'll explore key features like media integration, ecommerce, mailing lists, and social media that musicians should consider for their sites. We'll compare the pros and cons of built-in vs third party options. You'll learn how to align features with your audience, music genre, and business objectives. Let's dive in!

Core Features Musicians Should Consider

Today's website platforms offer a vast array of features to help musicians increase engagement, conversions, and revenue. Here are some core features worth considering:

Media Integration

Seamlessly showcase your music catalog and videos directly on your site through built-in integration or plugins.

Pros:

- Lets fans stream/download music
- Showcase videography and concert footage
- Demonstrate musical range and talents

Cons:

- Streaming costs and bandwidth requirements
- Needs regular updating as catalog grows

Ecommerce

Sell physical and digital merchandise through a full-featured store that integrates with order management and fulfillment.

Pros:

- Direct source of revenue
- Caters to fans who want to support you
- Sell special limited-edition merchandise

Cons:

- Inventory and shipping logistics
- Customer service expectations
- Additional transaction fees

Mailing List

Collect email addresses to send out newsletters, promotions, and exclusive content.

Pros:

- Owned audience communication channel

- Increase engagement and loyalty

- Promote new releases and events

Cons:

- Managing list hygiene and deliverability

- Time investment for quality emails

- Anti-spam compliance

Social Media Integration

Embed social feeds and share site content out to social platforms.

Pros:

- Expand reach and drive referral traffic

- Showcase multimedia content natively

- Curate highlights and previews

Cons:

- Content can quickly become outdated

- Privacy concerns around data usage

- Can detract from focused user experience

Let's explore more advanced capabilities to take your site to the next level.

Moving Beyond the Basics: Advanced Integrations

Once core features are implemented, musicians can augment their sites with advanced capabilities to drive deeper fan engagement and provide richer experiences.

Fan Forums / Communities

Dedicated subdomains or built-in forums for fans to interact, discuss music, and get to know each other.

Pros:

- Fosters loyalty and engagement

- Source of insight into fan interests

- Platform for exclusive content

Cons:

- Requires active moderation

- Hosting costs for activity spikes

- Fragmenting conversations

Presave Campaigns

Allow fans to presave upcoming song releases which automatically add to their playlists when released.

Pros:

- Build anticipation for new music

- Improves opening day streaming numbers

- Email capture for marketing

Cons:

- Complex integration with DSPs

- Need large existing audience

- Messaging risks overhyping

Virtual Reality

Immersive musical experiences for fans using VR apps and bidirectional livestreams.

Pros:

- Provides highly differentiated experiences

- Opportunity for virtual merchandise

- Deeper emotional fan connections

Cons:

- Still niche audience reach

- Technical complexity to implement

- Costly to produce quality experiences

Comparing Built-In vs Third-Party Options

Should you rely on integrated tools or third-party plugins? Here's an overview of the pros and cons:

Built-In Features

Pros:

- Tighter platform integration

- Unified design and UX

- Single account and billing

- Streamlined troubleshooting

Cons:

- More limited selection

- Less flexibility or customization

- Dependent on vendor roadmap

Third-Party Add-Ons

Pros:

- Wider range of niche options

- Ability to replace if needed

- Specialization leads to better support

- Often more customizable

Cons:

- Fragmented experiences

- Multiple logins required

- Higher risk of conflicts

- Security vulnerabilities

Evaluate your priorities - simplicity vs flexibility. Built-in features facilitate cohesion while third-parties enable broader customization.

Selecting Features Based on Music Genre

Certain website features align better to specific music genres' priorities.

Rock & Pop - Prioritize social integration and multimedia

Integrate Twitter and Instagram feeds to give fans a glimpse into your lives. Show behind-the-scenes clips on YouTube and TikTok. Allow instant song streaming.

Country & Folk - Focus on storytelling and mailing lists

Share lyrics explanations, studio vlogs, and images that provide context. Provide many ways to sign up for email newsletters. Send exclusive stories and content.

EDM & Dance - Drum up hype with presave campaigns

Time presave campaigns and AR filters to build anticipation for upcoming releases. Share teaser clips from DJ sets and festivals.

Hip Hop & Rap - Build engaged communities

Launch forums for discussing influences, lyrics, and culture. Enable social sharing of controversial topics. Share Spotify playlists and reactions.

Classical & Jazz - Immerse fans with multimedia

Upload past concert performances. Create VR environments for enjoying music. Provide high-fidelity streaming audio. Share images from venues and sets.

Aligning Business Goals with Website Features

Consider your objectives when selecting features.

Growth - Opt for social media integrations, mailing lists, and share prompts.

Engagement - Add communities, exclusives, contests, and opportunities to interact.

Promotion - Presave campaigns, multimedia samples, timely updates and teasers.

Revenue - Build out ecommerce, utilize affiliate programs, promote virtual events.

Data - Install analytics software, track mailing list metrics, integrate CRM.

These are just examples of how to map goals to potential features. You may have additional objectives to factor in.

Assessing Visitors to Determine Relevance

Take advantage of analytics to study your audience demographics and behaviors. This allows assessing which features will resonate best.

If visitors are mostly fans - focus on community, exclusives, and opportunities to connect.

If visitors are industry/press - share multimedia assets and EPK.

If visitors are general public - highlight social integration and sharing capabilities.

If visitors are recruiters - emphasize bio, skills, and brand messaging.

If visitors are venue bookers - showcase past performances, fan testimonials, and media praise.

Customizing experiences for different segments ensures you provide relevant features they actually want.

Comparing Website Builders Based on Key Features

Now that we've explored major features, how do top website builder platforms compare?

Wix

Wix has excellent built-in features like mailing lists, stores, and multimedia integration. But for advanced needs, third-party add-ons may be required. Ideal for blogs, portfolios and simple sites.

Squarespace

Squarespace enables beautiful multimedia content display and robust commerce capabilities out of the box. Expandable with advanced extensions. Great for content-focused sites.

Bandzoogle

Bandzoogle caters specifically to musicians with integrated tools for selling music, merch, and tickets. Decent built-ins but lacking advanced integrations.

WordPress

WordPress offers the most flexibility. Core features via plugins. Endless third-party integrations allow realizing any advanced functionality.

Shopify

Shopify specializes in ecommerce but integrates well with marketing and community plugins. Ideal for product-focused sites. Limited content capabilities.

This comparison shows top providers have strengths in different areas. Pick one that aligns best with your top priority features.

Comparing Pricing Considerations

Feature-rich plans on website builders usually come at a premium. Here are pricing factors to keep in mind:

- Number of product variants - more SKUs mean higher ecommerce plan

- Amount of online storage - videos, songs, and images require more space

- Desired email list size - bigger lists need upgraded plans

- Expected sales volumes - highermerchant processor fees

- Level of visitor traffic - bandwidth and infrastructure costs

- Integration add-ons - each extra plugin or app adds up

Study pricing carefully, but don't choose a plan strictly by cost alone. Make sure it can scale with your goals. Cheaper plans with low ceilings can cost more long term when you outgrow them quickly.

Pitfalls and Mistakes to Avoid

Building a feature-rich website involves some key pitfalls to avoid:

- Overestimating needed features - Start lean and add based on data.

- Signing long-term contracts - Choose flexible plans as needs evolve.

- Overbuilding before having an audience - Wait to have sufficient users and segments.

- Ignoring performance impacts - Fancy features can slow down site speed.

- Enabling too many social feeds - Curate to avoid cluttering experience.

- Choosing fad features without a clear purpose - Ensure relevance to goals.

By learning from these mistakes, you can take a measured approach to provide visitors the optimal experience.

Real-World Examples of Musicians' Websites

Let's look at some real-world examples of musicians effectively utilizing key website features.

mntrmusic.com

This electronic duo makes excellent use of multimedia showcasing their catalog. Their site conveys their futuristic vibe through sleek design. Presave campaigns on their homepage help build excitement for upcoming releases.

lizzomusic.com

Lizzo's site vibrantly reflects her colorful personality. Her media integrations showcase her singing, rapping, and flute talents. Shop integrations let fans sport her signature styles. Social feeds give candid behind-the-scenes looks.

alisonkrauss.com

Alison Krauss's new site redesign features a timeline of her storied career. The multimedia section provides many songs, videos, and images. A mailing list signup popup captures new subscribers. Her tour calendar highlights upcoming performances.

Each example aligns site features tightly to the artist's brand, music style, and fanbase preferences. Use these for inspiration when planning your own site.

Key Takeaways and Next Steps

Choosing the right website features involves careful planning:

- Identify must-have capabilities aligned to your goals

- Study analytics to understand your audience and their interests

- Map desired features to your music genre priorities

- Weigh pros and cons of built-in vs third-party options

- Select features that provide the best long-term value to your career

By following this process, you can provide fans, industry, and the general public an experience tailored specifically to resonate with them. Bring your vision to reality with the perfect set of features that represent your musical identity.

The next step is to pick a website platform that offers the functionality you need. Take advantage of free trials to test top options firsthand with temporary sites. Collaborate with their support teams during onboarding.

With strategic planning, you can launch a website equipped with the ideal features to share your music, promote your brand, foster connections, and propel your music career upward.

Summary

Media Integration

Pros	Cons
Lets fans stream/download music	Streaming costs and bandwidth requirements
Showcase videography and concert footage	Needs regular updating as catalog grows
Demonstrate musical range and talents	

E-commerce

Pros	Cons
Direct source of revenue	Inventory and shipping logistics
Caters to fans who want to support you	Customer service expectations
Sell special limited-edition merchandise	Additional transaction fees

Mailing List

Pros	Cons
Owned audience communication channel	Managing list hygiene and deliverability
Increase engagement and loyalty	Time investment for quality emails
Promote new releases and events	Anti-spam compliance

Social Media Integration

Pros	Cons
Expand reach and drive referral traffic	Content can quickly become outdated
Showcase multimedia content natively	Privacy concerns around data usage
Curate highlights and previews	Can detract from focused user experience

Built-In Features

Pros	Cons
Tighter platform integration	More limited selection
Unified design and UX	Less flexibility or customization
Single account and billing	Dependent on vendor roadmap
Streamlined troubleshooting	

Third-Party Add-Ons

Pros	Cons
Wider range of niche options	Fragmented experiences
Ability to replace if needed	Multiple logins required
Specialization leads to better support	Higher risk of conflicts
Often more customizable	Security vulnerabilities

Chapter 4

How to Make Your Music Website Easy to Use

Introduction

A musician's website must balance aesthetics and functionality. Beautiful designs mean nothing if fans struggle to use your site. An intuitive, seamless user experience is crucial.

In this chapter, we explore best practices for usability, accessibility, navigation, search, mobile optimization, and testing. You'll learn how to craft website interactions tailored to your fans' needs and preferences. Let's dive in!

Crafting an Intuitive Website Experience

Usability focuses on ensuring visitors can accomplish their goals on your site through intuitive interactions. Here are key elements to optimize:

Simplicity

Avoid clutter and confusion. Use clear messaging focused on primary calls-to-action.

Scannability

Facilitate skimming with quality headings, short paragraphs, and bulleted lists.

Consistency

Maintain unified navigation, UI elements, terminology, and styling across all pages.

Responsiveness

Provide instant feedback to user actions like form submissions, link clicks, etc.

Accessibility

Enable access for all users regardless of disabilities through semantics, color contrast, captions, etc.

These principles make your website effortless to use for every visitor. Let's look at specific tactics.

Improving Website Navigation and Architecture

Logical information architecture and navigation empower users to quickly find what they need.

Site Architecture Best Practices

- Organize content in intuitive categories users expect

- Use appropriately descriptive page titles and headings

- Link related content across sections for discoverability

- Structure pages in order of importance to users

- Ensure critical information is reachable within 3 clicks

Navigation Best Practices

- Use conventional top or left navigation schemes

- Limit primary nav links to 7 +/- 2 for usability

- Include search bar in main menu for easy access

- Make current page indicators obvious

- Use hierarchy of global, local, contextual navigation

With sound architecture and navigation, visitors remain oriented rather than lost.

Enhancing Discoverability Through Search

On-site search helps visitors instantly find relevant pages and content.

Pros	Cons
Users increasingly expect search	Adds development and maintenance overhead
Quick access to buried pages/content	Potentially costly depending on solution
Supplements navigation limitations	Requires search engine optimization expertise
Provides convenience and flexibility	Can divert users from curated paths

Follow these tips to maximize effectiveness:

- Optimize pages, metadata, and markup for search crawlability

- Analyze search queries to identify needed content improvements

- Provide autocomplete and suggested results

- Prioritize results by relevance over popularity/recency

- Position search bar prominently in header navigation

With performant search, users can self-serve the content they need.

Optimizing for Mobile and Touch Interactions

With over 60% of website traffic now on mobile devices, optimizing for smaller screens and touch interactions is critical.

Pros	Cons
Caters to majority of users and growing trend	Complexity of responsive multi-device development
Improves search rankings as Google prioritizes mobile-friendly sites	Potential need to limit some functionality on mobile
Enables on-the-go use for busy and traveling fans	Reflowing content can impact curated narrative flow
Allows engaging via social media and messaging on phones	Responsive retrofitting older sites has challenges

Best practices include:

- Simplified, intuitive navigation and menus

- Tap targets spaced at least 8mm apart

- Input elements sized appropriately for fingers

- Auto-expanding text fields

- Minimal horizontal scrolling

- High contrast buttons and controls

- Page speed optimization

By embracing mobile capabilities, you remove usage barriers anytime, anywhere.

Conducting Usability Testing with Real Users

Rigorously test your site with real representative users to identify usability issues.

Pros	Cons
Reveals pain points and friction unclear to site owners	Organizing participants and testing logistics requires effort
Quantifies through performance metrics like task completion rates	Need to offer incentives to secure participation
Captures subjective feedback directly from users	Interpreting and prioritizing divergent user opinions can prove difficult

| Builds empathy and understanding of visitor challenges | Testing budget and time constraints could limit insights gained |

Approaches for usability testing:

- Moderated - observe as participants complete preset tasks and think aloud

- Unmoderated - users complete tasks on live site independently and provide feedback afterward

- A/B testing - measure performance differences between variants

- Intercept surveys - get immediate feedback from site visitors

- Analytics analysis - identify problem areas based on real visitor behaviors

Iteratively testing with real users provides invaluable insights to incrementally refine site usability over time.

Driving Accessibility for All Fans

Ensure your website accommodates users of all abilities through ADA compliant accessibility practices:

Semantic HTML - Use proper tags for navigation, content, forms, etc. so screen readers can interpret them

ARIA attributes - Further enhance elements with roles, states and properties

Keyboard navigation - All functionality operable without mouse dependency

Color contrast - Minimum 4.5:1 contrast ratio between text and background

Alt text - Concise descriptions for images to explain to visually impaired users

Captions - Provide text transcripts for audio and video content

By making these practices part of your web development process, you remove barriers facing many potential fans.

Avoiding Common Pitfalls and Mistakes

Steer clear of these common usability pitfalls:

- Overly long, scrolling homepages hiding critical content

- Text-heavy pages without visual hierarchy

- Overuse of carousels, pop-ups, videos that distract

- Non-descriptive link names like "Click Here"

- Non-standard navigation patterns

- Blocking accessibility features

- Lack of mobile optimization

Putting in the effort to ensure usability pays dividends through greater user satisfaction, conversion rates, and fan retention.

Real-World Examples of Highly Usable Sites

Let's explore real-world music website examples with stellar usability and accessibility.

Alicia Keys - aliciakeys.com

Alicia Keys' site instantly engages visitors with striking visuals and intuitive navigation leading users to explore her music, videos, art, philanthropy and more. Sleek animations and transitions between sections provide a flawless user experience.

Shawn Mendes - shawnmendes.com

Shawn Mendes' website focuses on multimedia content with music and video seamlessly integrated. The image and video galleries showcase his talents while maintaining high performance. Clean typography and ample negative space keep the experience distraction-free.

Imogen Heap - imogenheap.com

Imogen Heap's creative site visually matches her innovative musical style. Playful animations and whimsical illustrations engage users while maintaining ease of use. The responsive design effortlessly adapts across mobile, tablet, and desktop.

Key Takeaways

Creating an optimal user experience involves:

- Structuring intuitive navigation and architecture

- Facilitating on-site search to improve discoverability

- Catering to mobile devices and touch interactions

- Ensuring accessibility for disabled users

- Iteratively testing with real representative users

By making your website effortless and enjoyable to use, you remove all friction distracting from fans connecting with your music.

Conclusion

Usability and accessibility can't be an afterthought. They must be central priorities when designing your music website. Treat your website as another extension of your art to evoke emotions through seamless interactions. By relentlessly focusing on user needs, you craft fulfilling experiences converting all visitors into loyal fans.

Chapter 5

Designing Your Music Website for Maximum Impact

Introduction

A website's visual design directly impacts users' perceptions of a musician's brand and artistic identity. An effectively designed site can grab attention, convey emotions, and immerse fans in your style.

In this chapter, we explore core principles for maximizing your website's visual impact. You'll learn how to express your musical personality through color, typography, layouts, imagery, and more. Let's dive in!

Fundamental Principles for Impactful Design

Several key principles form the foundation of highly effective music website design:

Simplicity - Eliminate clutter and overwhelm by strictly featuring only essential elements.

Scannability - Use visual hierarchy, whitespace, and concise copy for easy skimming.

Contrast - Create distinction between elements with strategic use of color, size, weight, and negative space.

Alignment - Use consistent grid systems to cleanly align page components.

Visual Impact - Make immersive first impressions with striking imagery, graphics, animation, and video.

Responsiveness - Craft adaptable designs that maintain impact on any device.

Accessibility - Enable access for all through color contrast, screen reader tags, captions, and semantics.

When these principles harmonize cohesively, websites become magnets attracting and engaging fans.

Defining Your Music Website Style Guide

Style guides document design systems, serving as blueprints for visual consistency. They should cover:

Color Palette - Primary and secondary colors that reflect your musical brand.

Typography - Font styles, sizes, and colors for headlines, body text, etc.

Graphic Elements - Illustrations, icons, logos, and other recurring visuals.

Image Style - Filters, editing guidelines, aspect ratios, etc. to unify imagery.

Sample Layouts - Compositions and grid systems to replicate across templates.

With well-defined style guides, websites maintain recognizable identities throughout.

Crafting Mobile-First Responsive Designs

With over 60% of traffic now from mobile, mobile-first design is imperative. This means structuring interfaces for mobile using progressive enhancement to layer in enhanced experiences on larger screens.

Benefits of mobile-first:

- Naturally focuses on simpler, more usable interfaces

- Avoids unnecessary clutter that can accumulate on larger screens

- Lightweight base experiences load faster on all devices

- Encourages designing for most constrained use cases

Tips for effective responsive design:

- Simplify navigation for small screens

- Size touch targets appropriately

- Adaptive media for smaller bandwidth

- Seamless transitions between breakpoints

- Maintain style guide consistency

- Avoid horizontal scrolling on mobile

With mobile-first methodology, impactful designs scale to any device or browser.

Selecting the Right Fonts and Typography

Typography profoundly impacts aesthetics and readability. Follow these best practices when selecting fonts:

- Limit to 2-3 complementary fonts - one for headings, one for body text

- Verify fonts work well together through typographic hierarchies

- Choose easily readable font faces for lengthy body text

- Use stylistic fonts sparingly for short-form highlighting

- Ensure ADA compliance with 4.5:1 minimum contrast ratios

- Accommodate translations with multilingual font support

Properly formatted typography facilitates scannability through:

- Clear visual hierarchy and styles showing relative importance

- Generous line heights for comfortable reading

- Short paragraphs with breathing room

- Bulleted lists for quick scanning

- Bold keywords and useful links for skimming

Strategic typography makes powerful first impressions.

Using the Right Colors for Your Brand

Color profoundly impacts aesthetics, emotions, and brand associations. Follow these guidelines when selecting colors:

- Limit to 2-3 primary colors that represent your musical identity and style

- Ensure enough contrast between background and text colors

- Use accent colors sparingly to highlight interactive elements

- Check colors work together through color mixing to avoid clashing

- Consider cultural color symbolism and meanings for your target markets

- Enable user option to invert color schemes for accessibility

Tools like Adobe Color can generate palettes complementary to your primary brand colors. Properly used color reinforces connections with fans.

Creating Page Layouts for Visual Impact

Layout distributes visual elements across space to establish visual hierarchy, flow, and focal points. Use these techniques:

- Structure layouts using grid systems and columns for alignment

- Frame key elements prominently according to their priority

- Use whitespace and margins to reduce crowding and create breathing room

- Maintain stylistic and functional consistency across page templates

- Use directional cues like arrows, color gradients, and lines to guide visitors through intended paths

- Adapt layouts rhythmically across breakpoints to retain impact on all devices

With strategic layouts, you guide visitors to immerse themselves in your music and brand story.

Showcasing Your Personality Through Imagery

Photos, illustrations, and videos uniquely show your musical identity and connect with fans. Images should:

- Feature recognizable elements of your artistic persona and style

- Use natural expressions rather than overly posed or stock photography

- Prioritize candid behind-the-scenes moments that reveal your authentic self

- Capture you focused on musical passions, whether performing or creative process

- Display visually stunning compositions and cinematography reflecting your aesthetic tastes

Ensure all imagery maintains stylistic consistency in editing, filters, aspect ratios, etc. Photos give fans an intimate look at your world.

Stimulating Emotion Through Animation and Video

Subtle animations and video immerse visitors in motion-rich experiences full of energy and emotion:

Pros	Cons
Draw attention and make strong first impressions	Overuse can increase development complexity
Allow creatively showcasing your musical talents	Performance impacts if not properly optimized

| Stimulate excitement and hype for new releases | Accessibility considerations around motion sickness |
| Guide visitors through intended journeys | Videos require significantly more production resources |

Best practices:

- Use animations purposefully to direct attention or transitions

- Videos should tell compelling stories complementing your brand

- Optimize encoding and compression for performance

- Allow user controls like pause, speed adjustment, and captions

When balanced well, motion engages fans far beyond static imagery.

Conveying Your Vision Through Conceptual Metaphors

Conceptual metaphors use symbolic imagery and language to convey intangible ideas. Music websites can highlight conceptual metaphors for your artistic vision through:

- Background graphics and illustrations

- Stylized photography manipulating subjects and environments

- Symbolic props, costumes, and set pieces

- Artistic media like drawings, paintings, graphic art

- Evocative poetic language and sensory details

For example, an electronic musician could use circuit board and futuristic technology patterns styled with technological glitch effects to reflect transhumanist themes.

By mapping visuals to your deeper creative concepts, you craft truly meaningful experiences.

Showcasing Your Media Style Through Website Aesthetics

Your website presents opportunities to feature all your artistic media and talents.

For photographers - Display striking portfolios.

For videographers - Showcase cinematic videos.

For painters - Exhibit galleries of artwork.

For graphic designers - Highlight original illustrations.

For fashion designers - Model your signature styles.

For lyricists - Publish compelling lyrics.

Ensure your website reinforces, rather than competes with, the impact of your core creative outputs. It should feel like an integrated artistic experience.

Avoiding Pitfalls of Ineffective Design

Steer clear of common music website design mistakes:

- Cliché overused templates and stale themes

- Distracting, chaotic clutter obscuring focus

- Overwhelming walls of unstructured text

- Mismatched aesthetic styles across pages

- Stock imagery that lacks authenticity

- Anything not clearly aligned with your brand identity

By maintaining relentless focus on core design principles and your creative vision, you craft truly differentiated websites that pop.

Real-World Examples of Impactful Music Sites

Let's explore examples of music websites exhibiting stellar design:

Billie Eilish - billieeilish.com

Billie Eilish's website immediately intrigues visitors with slowly animating conceptual imagery that sucks them into her dark, ethereal style. The visual language echoes her music videos with eerie environmental scenes and distressed glitch effects.

Ed Sheeran - edsheeran.com

Ed Sheeran's design features hand-drawn doodle illustration styles true to his personality. Vivid colors and playful animations crafted in his likeness complement his uplifting music to create an experience overflowing with life.

Imagine Dragons - imaginedragonsmusic.com

Imagine Dragons websites employ bold colors, grungy textures, and dynamic animations reflecting the intense energy of their alternative rock music. Their iconic logo stylized across visuals reinforces consistent branding.

Key Takeaways

Design your website for maximum impact through:

- Simple, scannable layouts optimized for mobile

- Illustrative colors, typography, and photography reflecting your style

- Animations and video that immerse fans in your vision

- Cohesive branding across all elements and pages

- Stylistic conceptual metaphors symbolizing your artistic ideas

With strategic design, your website becomes a visually stunning extension of your musical identity - an artistic experience in itself.

Conclusion

A musician's website design should grab attention and captivate fans just as profoundly as an album cover or music video. Treat it as a creative medium to showcase the essence of your musical brand. Hold your website's visuals to the same high standards as the rest of your creative output.

By harnessing core design principles and your unique style, you can craft website experiences as memorable and inspiring as your music. Your website design ultimately makes first impressions - ensure it immediately intrigues visitors to dive deeper into your artistic world.

Chapter 6

Incorporating an Events Calendar and Contact Form

Introduction

Musicians need easy ways for fans to learn about upcoming shows and get in touch. An events calendar and contact form provide these core functionalities.

In this chapter, we'll explore beginner-friendly options for adding these elements to your website. You'll learn how to create simple calendars displaying your tour dates, gigs, and appearances. We'll also cover basic contact forms so fans can reach you for booking inquiries, media requests, or questions. Let's get started!

Getting Started with Events Calendars

An events calendar allows you to share schedules of your upcoming performances, appearances, release parties, signings, and other happenings with fans and industry folks. By providing a way to see your events at-a-glance in one place, you make it easier for people to learn about opportunities to see you live and potentially attend.

Here are some key reasons calendars are important:

- Promote your shows and drive ticket sales

- Allow fans to discover when you're performing near them

- Help industry like talent buyers efficiently scout you

- Build excitement and hype for special events

- Demonstrate your busy performance schedule

Now let's look at simple ways to add calendars without advanced skills.

Using Built-In Calendar Widgets

Many website builders like Wix and Squarespace include built-in calendar widgets you can add. These provide easy interactive calendars without needing to code:

- Simply search for calendar in the widgets panel

- Drag and drop the calendar onto any page

- Configure settings like colors and fonts

- Add your events with details like dates, locations, links

- Visitors can browse and click events

Pros:

- Extremely easy "plug and play" installation

- Handles calendars functionality out of the box

- Matches site styles and branding by default

Cons:

- Limited customization options

- Events may not automatically sync across other calendars

- Widget placement restrictions can apply

Using Shared Calendars from Gmail or iCloud

Another beginner option is embedding a shared calendar from your free accounts like Gmail or iCloud:

- Create a calendar in your existing account and add events

- Find the sharing or embed feature to get an embed code

- Add the embed code to your site page HTML using your builder's code module

- The calendar syncs automatically when you update events

Pros:

- Simple way to display calendars you're already using

- Changes sync automatically across devices

- Free and easy to set up

Cons:

- Basic branding and customization options

- Cluttered if you have many other calendars

- Service provider ads may show

These simple approaches allow easily displaying events without calendar website integration hurdles. But for advanced customization, let's look at popular calendar platforms.

Integrating Advanced Calendar Platforms

For greater customization and synchronization across your website, mailing lists, and other promotion channels, dedicated calendar platforms are the best option. Popular choices like Bandsintown, Gigwell, and Songkick offer convenient integration.

Here's an overview of how they work:

- Create calendar on platform and add your events

- Install their app or export API feed to your website

- Embedded calendar syncs automatically

- Fans can follow you and get alerts about events

- Promote your calendar URL for discoverability

Pros:

- Endlessly customizable designs and views

- Automatic syncing across platforms

- Advanced features like RSVPs, maps, tickets

- Dedicated apps make updating easy

Cons:

- Steeper learning curve

- Potential costs depending on features needed

- Manual installation of apps or API required

- Dependent on third-party platform

While more complex, dedicated calendars give you total control to match your brand style.

Promoting Your Calendar

To maximize visibility, promote your calendar URL across:

- Your website footer

- Email newsletter and autoresponder sign-up flows

- Social media bios and posts

- Printed materials like flyers, posters, merch

- Press and media kits or EPKs

- Direct mailing lists and street teams

Encourage fans to follow or import your calendar into their own calendars for automated event reminders. Consider giving perks like pre-sale access for early subscribers.

Making Your Calendar Mobile-Friendly

With many users now on mobile, ensure your calendar is optimized for small screens:

- Use simple, clean designs avoiding clutter

- Size touch targets for fingertips

- Test interactions like date pickers work easily

- Minimize need for zooming and horizontal scrolling

- Adapt layouts for vertical scrolling on phones

- Ensure fast page load speeds on cellular

Mobile-friendliness helps fans conveniently discover and share your events on-the-go.

Allowing Fans to Export or Embed Your Calendar

Maximize shareability by adding embed codes or export links:

- Export to CSV or ICAL formats fans can download

- Provide HTML snippets fans can embed on their own sites

- Add share buttons for easy social posting

The more your calendar spreads through fan networks organically, the greater the exposure.

Avoiding Common Calendar Mistakes

Steer clear of these pitfalls when creating your events calendar:

- Forgetting to update with new events

- Burying the calendar under confusing navigation

- Cluttering with excessive non-event information

- Leaving dead links if event pages get removed

- Not optimizing calendar for mobile

- Blocking ability to export or embed the calendar

- Missing key details like venue, times, ticket links

By keeping your calendar clean, accessible, and updated, you ensure fans can always easily stay in the loop on happenings.

Adding a Contact Form to Your Website

Now let's explore easy ways to let fans get in touch by adding a contact form to your site.

Why You Need a Contact Form

A contact form provides an essential channel for visitors to reach you directly through your website. Here are key reasons to offer a form:

- Allow fans to send fan mail, questions, or feedback

- Receive booking inquiries from talent buyers

- Get media requests from journalists and bloggers

- Enable easy merch ordering by receives

- Let fans report issues with your site or submit bugs

- Provide a way to request autographs or other favors

Without a form, you force visitors to hunt for your email across social media channels. A form makes contacting straightforward.

Picking a Contact Form Service

Many user-friendly services provide ready-made contact form building and management:

Popular options:

- Formspree (free for up to 1,000 submissions per month)

- FormKeep (starting at $9 per month)

- FormGet (starting at $14 per month)

- FormSubmit (free version with branding)

- FormAssembly (starting at $29 per month)

These tools make it easy to create custom forms with no coding, while handling spam filtering and responses.

Creating Your Form

Most form builders provide simple drag-and-drop editors:

- Pick form fields - like name, email, subject, and message

- Customize design - themes, colors, fonts, etc.

- Add validation - prevent blank submissions

- Enable CAPTCHA - stops bots with puzzles

- Set up notifications - get emails when receiving submissions

- Publish form code snippet on your site

Pro Tips:

- Keep fields brief focusing only on essentials

- Use user-friendly inputs like radio buttons over long menus

- Show user-friendly error messages if validation fails

- Allow file uploads for media and press kits

Optimizing Form Accessibility

Ensure your form complies with accessibility standards:

- Use correct HTML form element semantics

- Set keyboard tab order logically

- Proper ARIA labels describing non-text elements

- Sufficient color contrast for the visually impaired

- Review screen reader pronunciation and descriptions

Accessibility enables all visitors to successfully use your form.

Promoting Your Contact Form

Make your form discoverable by linking to it prominently:

- Link in website header or footer navigation

- Embed on contact and press kit pages

- Promote on email list and social media

- Provide contact form URL for press inquiries

- Include link in PDF press kits and one sheets

The easier you make your form to find, the more contacts you'll receive.

Managing Form Submissions and Responding

Check and respond to submissions regularly so contacts don't go missed:

- Configure email notifications of new submissions

- Set up rules and labels to route messages to appropriate folders

- Export submissions to CSV/Excel for tracking and analysis

- Craft template responses where appropriate

- Follow-up with website form fillers to build loyalty

Prompt replies encourage further engagement with new fans and contacts.

Avoiding Common Form Mistakes

Sidestep these contact form pitfalls:

- Asking for excessive personal information

- No confirmation messages upon submitting

- Not auto-responding to acknowledge receipts

- Letting submissions go unmonitored and unanswered

- Blocking emails from domains and spamming legitimate users

- Using cryptic category names like "Type of Inquiry"

- Forcing users to re-enter information that was already provided

Keep your forms focused, friendly, and functional above all.

Key Takeaways

We covered beginner steps for adding events calendars and contact forms:

- Use simple built-in widgets from site builders

- Embed calendars from existing accounts

- Explore advanced integrations like Bandsintown

- Promote your calendar across all channels

- Choose user-friendly contact form services

- Follow accessibility and promotion best practices

- Monitor submissions and respond promptly

With functional calendars and contact forms, fans can easily discover events and reach you from your website.

Summary of pros and cons

Using Built-In Calendar Widgets

Pros	Cons
Extremely easy "plug and play" installation	Limited customization options
Handles calendars functionality out of the box	Events may not automatically sync across other calendars
Matches site styles and branding by default	Widget placement restrictions can apply

Using Shared Calendars from Gmail or iCloud

Pros	Cons
Simple way to display calendars you're already using	Basic branding and customization options
Changes sync automatically across devices	Cluttered if you have many other calendars
Free and easy to set up	Service provider ads may show

Integrating Advanced Calendar Platforms

Pros	Cons
Endlessly customizable designs and views	Steeper learning curve
Automatic syncing across platforms	Potential costs depending on features needed
Advanced features like RSVPs, maps, tickets	Manual installation of apps or API required
Dedicated apps make updating easy	Dependent on third-party platform

Conclusion

Providing convenient ways for fans to learn about your schedule and contact you fosters deeper engagement. Keep calendars and forms well-maintained and prominently promoted. Treat all inquiries and outreach with respect. With ongoing nurturing of contacts generated, your website becomes a thriving hub strengthening bonds with your audience.

Chapter 7

Integrating Social Media into Your Music Website

Introduction

Social media is essential for musicians to expand their reach and engage with fans. Integrating social platforms into your website keeps visitors connected and informed.

This chapter explores effective strategies to incorporate social media on your site. You'll learn best practices for displaying social profiles, embedding feeds, and enabling social sharing. Let's get started!

Linking to Your Social Profiles

Enabling visitors to easily access your social profiles from your website fosters discovery across networks.

Best practices for adding social media links:

- Place icons prominently in the header or footer navigation menus. This gives persistent access from all pages.

- Use official brand icons for recognizability.

- Link icons to the main profile URLs for each platform.

- Only include actively used platforms relevant to your audience. Avoid outdated or irrelevant links.

- Arrange icons in order of importance based on where you are most active and fans expect to find you.

- Make icons large enough to clearly convey the brands, but don't distract from other navigation. Sizes between 24px-32px are ideal.

- Have icons open profiles in new browser tabs so visitors remain on your site.

Prominent yet unobtrusive social media links retain visitor attention while enabling discovery.

Embedding Social Media Feeds

Embedding selectively curated social feeds directly into your website content keeps visitors engaged. Evaluate adding embedded feeds for:

- Major announcements and releases - Share your posts highlighting new music, merch, tour dates, etc.

- Rich media - Display vibrant photos, videos, and audio from events, studio updates, behind-the-scenes glimpses, and performances.

- Interactions - Showcase replies and engagement with fans to highlight your accessibility.

- Reviews and reactions - Embed posts praising your work and sharing success stories.

- Contests and promotions - Feature special offers and campaigns.

Pros:

- Provides dynamic, fresh content from social platforms.

- Saves visitors time by curating highlights so they don't have to dig through entire feeds.

- Allows showcasing content already being produced for social channels.

Cons:

- Can appear disjointed from rest of branded website experience.

- Content quickly becomes outdated and irrelevant if not maintained.

- Decreased control compared to fully owned content.

Balance embedded social content with sufficient original material produced specifically for your website.

Enabling Social Sharing

Make it easy for visitors to share your website content and spreads the word organically:

Sharing Buttons

- Add official sharing buttons for major platforms like Facebook, Twitter, Pinterest near page content.

- Maintain consistent positioning and styling across pages.

- Place buttons before bulk page content so users can share before reading/scrolling.

- Configure buttons to share the current URL, title, description, and image.

- Track shares with analytics to identify trending content.

Shareable Content

- Create inherently shareable content like personalized quizzes, widgets, calculators.

- Produce listicles, meme graphics, and infographics designed for social engagement.

- Maintain fresh, evergreen content so old material remains relevant to share.

- Write titles and descriptions optimized to entice social sharing.

Prompts

- Occasionally prompt visitors explicitly to share specific pages or content if you feel they are highly shareable.

- Segment visitors by behavior to target social sharing prompts to likely sharers.

Frictionless sharing extends your reach and saves promotional costs.

Driving Traffic from Social Media

You can also drive website traffic from social platforms through:

- Linking to your website content from social posts and profiles.

- Sharing content optimized for each platform - videos for TikTok, images for Instagram, snippets for Twitter.

- Cross-posting website article excerpts natively on social feeds.

- Leveraging social advertising to promote website offerings.

- Encouraging user-generated content and re-sharing.

- Using platforms like Linktree to showcase links.

- Promoting website offerings in live streams and events.

An integrated social promotion strategy maximizes referral traffic to your site.

Measuring Social Media ROI

Analyze social media performance and optimization opportunities through metrics like:

- Website referral traffic from social platforms

- Engagement with on-site social sharing buttons

- Conversions from site visits referred from social

- Follower growth and demographics on each platform

- Content resonance testing via A/B testing

- ROI from social advertising pointing visitors to site

Prove the value of social initiatives or identify areas for realignment based on data.

Key Takeaways

- Link prominent social media icons for discoverability.

- Curate social feeds to showcase highlights.

- Enable easy social sharing with buttons and prompts.

- Cross-promote website and social content across channels.

- Analyze performance to optimize social strategies.

An integrated social presence ultimately allows expanding your fanbase and engagement across the digital landscape.

Conclusion

Approached strategically, integrating social media into your website provides a vital avenue to extend your brand reach. But balance social content with an owned presence and original material on your site. Promote website offerings on social platforms and drive traffic back. Analyze efforts based on key metrics to continually refine your social presence and engagement.

Chapter 8

Building Your Music Website with AI

Introduction

Building a fully functional website used to require advanced coding skills. But artificial intelligence (AI) has changed that. Now, AI-powered tools allow anyone to create professional music websites without technical expertise.

This chapter explores beginner-friendly AI website builders tailored for musicians. We'll break down how AI assists with design, content creation, optimization, and more. You'll learn step-by-step workflows for assembling a complete website. Let's dive in!

Understanding AI Website Builders

Traditional website builders rely on complex manual processes like:

- Hard-to-use drag and drop editors or code.

- Finding and tweaking templates to match your brand.

- Writing and organizing all content from scratch.

- Manually adjusting designs for mobile optimization.

- Guessing effective page layouts and navigation.

AI website builders simplify this through automation:

- AI analyzes your style preferences to generate tailored templates.

- AI assists writing and arranging new content and copy.

- AI designs adapt seamlessly across desktop and mobile.

- AI optimizes page layouts, menus, and navigation automatically.

- AI provides easy customization suggestions to match your brand.

This allows easy creation of advanced sites without technical skills. Leading AI website builders for musicians include Wix ADI, WordPress Gutenberg Editor, SquareSpace, Duda, and more.

Benefits of AI Website Builders

AI provides many advantages for music site creation:

- Great sites in minutes with minimal effort.

- Easy drag-and-drop editing if desired.

- Takes brand style input to provide tailored designs.

- Generates original text content from prompts and keywords.

- Optimizes for search engines and speed automatically.

- Built-in mobile responsiveness without adjustments.

- Analyzes site usage to suggest improvements.

- Many essential features like contact forms, mailing lists, and galleries pre-integrated.

AI handles the heavy lifting so you focus on creative work and connecting with fans. Let's walk through the workflow.

Step-by-Step Guide to Building Your Site

Follow these steps to easily construct an AI-powered website:

Choose a builder

Research top AI website builders and select one fitting your budget and needs:

- Wix - extremely easy to use but less design flexibility.

- Squarespace - sophisticated templates with ample customization options.

- WordPress - open source with plugins enabling advanced features.

- Shopify - specifically for ecommerce stores but with expansive capabilities.

Start your free trial to test the builder hands-on.

Provide creative direction

Submit details to guide your site design:

- Share your color palette, fonts, and visual styles.

- Provide logos, icons, and sample imagery.

- Select preferred animations, layouts, and themes.

- Curate examples of sites you love.

- Submit marketing materials like your one sheet or press kit so the AI can analyze your brand.

Answer questions

The AI builder will ask questions to understand your goals, target audience, content needs and more:

- What is the purpose and focus of your site?

- What types of pages and sections do you need?

- What forms or functionality are required?

- Who is your ideal visitor persona?

- How do you want visitors to navigate the site?

Answer honestly so the AI can craft relevant experiences.

Review AI draft

The AI will generate an initial website draft incorporating your responses and direction. Critically review:

- Ensure the design aesthetically represents your brand identity.

- Confirm content and messaging resonates with your target fans.

- Verify key pages like About, Music, Shop, Events are included.

- Check forms and integrations function as needed.

- Ensure ease of navigation between sections.

Provide feedback to the AI to guide iterative improvements until satisfied.

Publish and customize

Once approved, publish your site! The AI builder streamlines further enhancement:

- Easily rearrange or add new pages and sections with drag and drop.

- Further tweak design and branding elements like fonts, colors, and imagery.

- Expand written content by providing additional text for the AI to incorporate.

- Add multimedia like music samples, videos, and photo galleries.

- Install additional features like forums, user reviews, or ecommerce.

- Activate built-in SEO tools to optimize visibility.

Leverage AI guidance to match your brand as you personalize.

Promote and maintain

With your site live, focus on promotion and care:

- Share your new site URL on social media, email lists, and press kits.

- Analyze site analytics to identify popular pages and opportunities.

- Monitor search engine rankings to improve visibility.

- Keep content updated, especially time-sensitive elements like tour dates.

- Use built-in AI suggestions to continually refine and enhance your presence.

Diligent promotion and care ensures your site always shines.

AI Page and Content Creation

Now let's explore AI website creation in more detail, starting with AI-generated pages and content.

AI-Powered Page Design

AI website builders design effective page layouts tailored to your brand:

- Analyzes your target audience and brand identity.

- Considers content types needed like text, multimedia, forms.

- Identifies optimal page structures based on goals.

- Designs stylistic templates matching your aesthetic.

- Adapts layouts responsively for all devices automatically.

- Continually experiments and optimizes based on visitor data.

This elevates beyond generic template choices to pages strategically designed just for you.

AI-Generated Content

AI can also assist generating engaging written content:

- Simply provide a topic, keywords, tone parameters.

- AI will research the subject and outline key points.

- AI will draft unique paragraphs and articles.

- Review AI drafts and provide directional feedback.

- AI improves content based on your revisions.

- Use AI drafts as starting points and edit further.

This provides abundant seed content to modify rather than writing from scratch.

Best Practices

Follow these tips for quality AI content:

- Provide detailed prompts indicating purpose, length, voice, and goals.

- Seed AI with your lyrics or writings so it learns your style.

- Ensure AI reflects your authentic perspective rather than generic tropes.

- Use AI for raw drafts still needing your review and nuanced refinement.

- Adapt finalized AI content across platforms like social media and email lists.

With thoughtful guidance, AI becomes an invaluable writing partner.

AI for Visuals, Data, and Code

AI can also generate and optimize visual components, data insights, and technical code.

Visual AI Creation

- Generates logos, images, and original graphics based on prompts.

- Creates variations to A/B test for optimal performance.

- Adapts imagery for different dimensions and formats needed.

- Optimizes photos and graphics for loading speed.

- Analyzes visual trends to recommend on-brand styles.

Data AI Insights

- Tracks detailed site analytics on traffic, engagement, conversions.

- Monitors user behaviors to identify pain points.

- Provides data-driven suggestions to improve performance.

- Optimizes page layouts, navigation, and configurations based on data.

- Predicts trends and future opportunities.

AI Code Generation

- Converts content models into underlying HTML markup.

- Provides SEO enhancements for speed and metadata optimization.

- Scans for and remedies accessibility issues in code.

- Identifies and fixes bugs and technical errors.

- Updates libraries and dependencies for smoother performance.

AI elevates creative opportunities while handling technical complexities.

Common Concerns and Considerations

Some common concerns around AI website builders include:

Creative constraints – Some feel AI restricts custom creative expression. However, most builders provide ample editing options after initial AI drafts. Think of AI as jumpstarting creativity rather than replacing it.

Impersonal experiences – Since AI generates standardized experiences, some worry they may seem impersonal. However, the more unique data you provide about your brand upfront, the better AI can deliver personalized results.

Cost – AI tools may have higher costs, but significant savings from easier development and boosted performance can offset this. Weigh costs vs immense time savings and revenue growth.

Learning curve – AI builders still have some learning curves. But they are far simpler than coding and many traditional manual processes required previously.

Control limitations – Some AI platforms restrict migrations or edits. Choose builders allowing custom domains, unlimited edits, transparent data ownership, and flexibility.

While valid considerations, the tremendous upsides AI provides make adoption well worthwhile.

Key Takeaways

In summary:

- AI website builders streamline creation without coding.

- They provide tailored templates, optimized layouts, and generated content.

- Follow the steps to input brand direction, review AI drafts, publish, and promote.

- AI accelerates and elevates website creation through data-driven insights.

- Thoughtfully embrace AI tools to enhance (not replace) your creative perspective.

Conclusion

AI-powered solutions provide game-changing opportunities for musicians seeking full creative control over polished websites that deeply resonate with fans. With the right strategic guidance, AI becomes an invaluable asset augmenting creativity rather than inhibiting it. Your website serves as a dynamic creative canvas showcasing the unique intersection of your musical vision and intelligent technology.

Chapter 9

Preparing to Market Your New Music Website

Launching your music website is a huge accomplishment, but the real work has just begun. Effective marketing determines whether your site sinks or swims.

This final chapter introduces the core strategies covered in-depth in the upcoming guide "Marketing Your Music Website: Proven Tactics to Drive Traffic, Engagement, and Revenue". Let's recap key concepts to prime your mindset before diving into the complete marketing blueprint.

Driving Website Traffic

Promote your site's URL across all channels - email lists, social media, live performances, press releases, collaborations, etc. Search engine optimization and partnerships will also increase discovery. Consistent marketing brings continuous new visitors.

Compelling Website Engagement

Quality content and community foster engagement. Personalized experiences tailored to each visitor also enhance stickiness. Multimedia, interactivity, and value-added content prevent bounce-backs. Optimizations based on analytics and testing maximize time on site.

Guiding Visitors to Conversions

Email capture, ecommerce sales, content downloads, event RSVPs, and subscriptions convert impressed visitors into invested fans. Streamline purchase and sign-up flows. Use promotions, calls-to-action, and perks to nudge conversions.

Evolving Your Website Over Time

Add fresh blogs, multimedia, features, and enhancements consistently to avoid going stale. Fix bugs quickly. Improve navigation and designs. Follow trends and best practices. Doubling down on what works accelerates success.

Safeguarding Your Website

Backupyour website regularly and store copies securely offsite. Install security protections like SSL, access controls, and DDoS mitigation. Scan for vulnerabilities. Test restores to ensure availability if disaster strikes.

As you can see, marketing requires both creativity and consistency. The upcoming guide expands on these concepts with concrete strategies and step-by-step blueprints. You'll learn proven tactics to:

- Build a responsive email list to tap anytime

- Create viral content that spreads socially

- Leverage search engine optimization for free discovery

- Promote your website through online and offline channels

- Foster an engaged user community

- Analyze data to guide decisions

- Monetize web traffic through diverse revenue streams

- Automate repetitive marketing tasks

- Test content and offers to maximize conversions

And more! With the right marketing foundations now in place, you're ready to fully capitalize on your website's potential.

So stay tuned for the next installment packed with hands-on music website marketing techniques to attract hordes of new fans, compel engagement, and propel your music career upward.

#	Action Item
1	Research leading AI website builders for musicians
2	Assess needs and budget to pick the right platform
3	Compare features, capabilities, and pricing of top website builders
4	Sign up for free trials of promising platforms
5	Select the builder that best fits your skills and goals
6	Make wishlist of must-have website features and functionality
7	Prioritize capabilities that align with your audience and goals
8	Determine if built-in tools suffice or if add-ons/plugins needed
9	Plan site architecture and navigation for intuitive user flows
10	Incorporate search functionality to aid discoverability

11	Optimize for mobile users and touch interactions
12	Conduct usability tests with real users for feedback
13	Compile brand style guide with visual assets, colors, and fonts
14	Curate examples of aesthetics and layouts you love
15	Select engaging imagery representing your musical identity
16	Balance visuals with ample negative space for focus
17	Add calendar widget or sync from existing calendar
18	Promote calendar URL across channels
19	Pick user-friendly contact form builder and customize
20	Make form accessible across site and in press kit
21	Link prominent social media icons in header/footer

22	Embed selectively curated social media feeds
23	Install sharing buttons for user-generated promotion
24	Provide detailed brand direction to guide AI site generation
25	Review and provide feedback on initial AI draft
26	Publish site then continue optimizing with AI guidance
27	Develop full marketing plan (see next guide)
28	Promote new site across email, social, collaborations
29	Analyze metrics to optimize content and flows
30	Add fresh material and features consistently